B 1/4/13 9/17

D0538773

*T1-AXV-055*

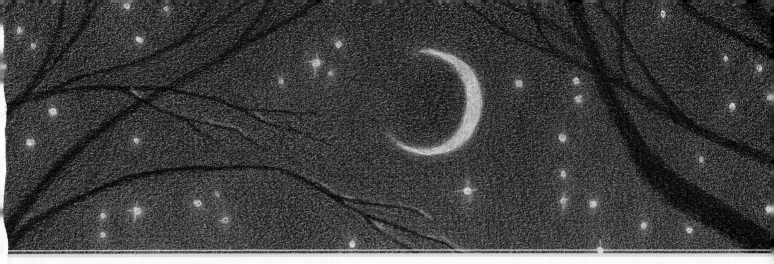

# LOOK UP!

*HENRIETTA LEAVITT,*
*PIONEERING WOMAN*
*ASTRONOMER*

ROBERT BURLEIGH          Illustrated by RAÚL COLÓN

A Paula Wiseman Book
SIMON & SCHUSTER BOOKS FOR YOUNG READERS

New York    London    Toronto    Sydney    New Delhi

*For Claudia—who loves to scan the sky at night*
*—R. B.*

*For Kate, Gaby, and Alice—stars in their own right*
*—R. C.*

SIMON & SCHUSTER BOOKS FOR YOUNG READERS
An imprint of Simon & Schuster Children's Publishing Division
1230 Avenue of the Americas, New York, New York 10020
Text copyright © 2013 by Robert Burleigh
Illustrations copyright © 2013 by Raúl Colón
SIMON & SCHUSTER BOOKS FOR YOUNG READERS is a trademark of Simon & Schuster, Inc.
For information about special discounts for bulk purchases, please contact Simon & Schuster Special Sales at 1-866-506-1949 or
business@simonandschuster.com.
The Simon & Schuster Speakers Bureau can bring authors to your live event. For more information or to book an event, contact the
Simon & Schuster Speakers Bureau at 1-866-248-3049 or visit our website at www.simonspeakers.com.
Book design by Laurent Linn
The text for this book is set in Diotima LT Std.
The illustrations for this book are rendered in watercolors, Prismacolor pencils, and lithograph pencils on Arches paper.
Manufactured in China • 1212 SCP
2  4  6  8  10  9  7  5  3  1
Library of Congress Cataloging-in-Publication Data
Burleigh, Robert.
Look up! : Henrietta Leavitt, pioneering woman astronomer / Robert Burleigh; illustrated by Raúl Colón.
p. cm.
"A Paula Wiseman Book."
ISBN 978-1-4169-5819-2 (hardcover)
ISBN 978-1-4424-8110-7 (eBook)
1. Leavitt, Henrietta Swan, 1868–1921—Juvenile literature. 2. Women astronomers—United States—Biography.
3. Astronomers—United States—Biography. I. Colón, Raúl, ill. II. Title.
QB36.L328B87 2010
520.92—dc22
[B]
2008029918

$N$ight after night, Henrietta sat on her front porch, gazing up at the stars.

*How high?*

*How high is the sky?*

She wanted to know everything about the wonderful bigness of all she saw. The more she looked up, the bigger the sky seemed to get. It seemed endless!

On cloudless evenings she found the Big Dipper, inching its slow glittering track across the night sky. She drew an imaginary line from the Dipper's pan.

*See, it leads to the North Star!*

Sometimes she felt the stars were trying to speak, to tell her what they knew.

When Henrietta was a young woman, almost all astronomy teachers and students were men.

In an astronomy class, she was one of the very few women students. But Henrietta wanted to follow what she loved, wherever it took her.

And most of all, she loved the sense of vast distances. Light-years! The distance that light can travel in one year—about six trillion miles! And many stars were light-years away. Think of it! Amazing!

After graduating, Henrietta worked in an observatory, where people studied the stars. In the observatory was a giant telescope. Even so, Henrietta seldom had a chance to gaze through it to see the stars up close.

Instead, she worked in a small room alongside other women. The hours were long and the pay was only thirty cents an hour. The women who worked there were human "computers."

Their job was to record. And measure. And calculate. The women were expected to "work, not think."

But Henrietta had other ideas.

Didn't she have a mind? And couldn't she use it? Each day she peered through a magnifying glass to measure tiny star dots on photographs of the previous night's sky. On the photographs, the stars resembled little bits of dust.

What could these tiny dots tell her? What were they saying?

Henrietta kept studying in her spare time. She read about the lives of the great astronomers. She loved to repeat to herself her favorite "sky-words": *asteroids, cosmic dust,* and *eclipse.*

Copernicus

galileo

At work she looked and looked and looked, until her eyes blurred. When she closed her eyes, she could still see the star dots, dancing across the inside of her eyelids.

Day after day there were new photographs of stars to look at. Day after day, Henrietta returned to the small, stuffy room and, together with the other women workers, studied the photographs. She measured. She took notes. She looked.

And looked.

And looked.

Slowly, she began to see tiny differences between the star dots.

She especially studied a group of stars that glowed and dimmed—and then glowed again. She even discovered some "blinking" stars that no one had ever discovered before! But there was still more to do. Patiently, Henrietta worked on.

She recorded the number of nights it took for each blinking star to go from dim to bright, or from "off to on."

One day she realized something. Some very bright stars blinked more slowly than the less bright stars. *What could this mean?* She began to keep a careful chart.

Suddenly, Henrietta saw a pattern!

A slow blink-time meant that a star contained lots of light power, or brightness. And if the blink-time was even slower, the star contained even more light. By measuring the time it took for a star to go from "off" to "on," one could tell the *true* brightness of any blinking star in the sky, even if it was just a faint speck, far, far away!

The head astronomer at the observatory was amazed. When astronomers know the *true* brightness of a star, it helps them figure out how far the star is from the Earth. Henrietta was onto something. A breakthrough!

*Yes, I am an astronomer!*

Henrietta published her chart in a magazine. She was proving that the smallest observation, the tiniest discovery, often leads to something very important.

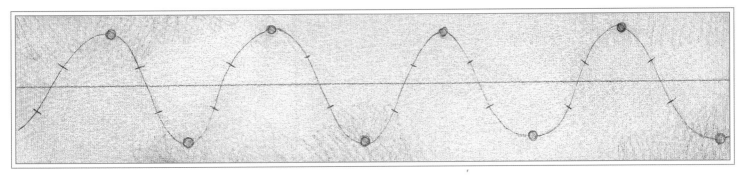

Around this time, most people thought the Milky Way, the galaxy containing the Earth, made up the whole universe. But not anymore.

Henrietta's chart helped astronomers measure distances much farther away. First, the Milky Way itself was found to stretch out farther than anyone thought.

Next, astronomers discovered even more galaxies—many of them. The universe was far more vast than anyone had ever dreamed!

The stars had spoken to Henrietta.

Still, she kept working. One winter night, walking home from the observatory, she stopped. The sky was cold and very clear.

She suddenly remembered her childhood, long ago, when she had gazed up from her parent's front porch.

*Yes, it is the same beautiful and mysterious sky—but now it is so much bigger!*

Henrietta smiled. Her mind roamed. She dreamed. She whispered to herself again.

*How high?*

*How high is the sky?*

# WHAT PEOPLE HAVE SAID ABOUT THE STARS

"The stars are suspended on strings that are pulled up in the daytime and let down at night."
—*Babylonian mythology*

"If you follow your star, you cannot fail to find a glorious heaven."
—*Dante Alighieri*

"When it is dark enough, you can see the stars."
—*Ralph Waldo Emerson*

"Today gives us a chance to love, to work, to play, and to look up at the stars."
—*Henry Van Dyke*

"As marvelous as the stars is the mind of the person who studies them."
—*Martin Luther King Jr.*

"We walk up the beach under the stars. And when we are tired of walking,
we lie flat on the sand under a bowl of stars."
—*Anne Morrow Lindbergh*

"The stars hang bright above, silent, as if they watched the sleeping earth."
—*Samuel Taylor Coleridge*

"The stars are the jewels of the night, and perchance surpass anything which day has to show."
—*Henry David Thoreau*

"For my part I know nothing with any certainty, but the sight of the stars makes me dream."
—*Vincent Van Gogh*

"I have loved the stars too fondly to be fearful of the night."
—*Sarah Williams*

"We all shine on, like the moon, and the stars, and the sun."
—*John Lennon*

"Keep your eyes on the stars, and your feet on the ground."
—*Theodore Roosevelt*

"Always remember, you have within you the strength, the patience,
and the passion to reach for the stars to change the world."
—*Harriet Tubman*

# AFTERWORD

HENRIETTA SWAN LEAVITT was born on July 4, 1868. Although she made a very important discovery in astronomy, not a great deal is known about her life. She had an early interest in astronomy, and she graduated from Radcliffe College in 1892. During her lifetime, however, women were mostly kept from doing key research in almost all the sciences.

Still, she worked for many years at the Harvard College Observatory in Cambridge, Massachusetts. Here, alongside other women, she was assigned the task of measuring star positions and sizes from photographs taken through the observatory's telescope.

It was while she was acting as a human "computer" that she discovered how certain stars—called Cepheid variable stars because their light varies, or glows and fades—had a fixed pattern to their changes.

Using the discovery made by Henrietta, astronomers were able—with the help of other facts and formulas—to measure greater and greater distances. This led to our present understanding of the vast size of the universe. An astronomer of her time called Henrietta Leavitt "one of the most important women ever to touch astronomy." Another close associate said she had the "best mind at the Harvard Observatory." A few years after she died in 1921, a famous astronomer even considered nominating her for the Nobel Prize.

# WHAT DID HENRIETTA LEAVITT DISCOVER?

Henrietta Leavitt helped discover the first accurate method for measuring great distances in space. Before Henrietta's time, scientists thought our galaxy, the Milky Way, was all there was to the universe. We now know (with Henrietta's and other scientists' help, as well as the assistance of larger telescopes) that the universe is far larger than anyone knew.

How did she do it? In 1902, Edward Pickering at the Harvard College Observatory hired Henrietta Leavitt and asked her to look at and compare photographs of stars, photographs taken each night at the Observatory. No one had a system for doing this, so Henrietta Leavitt developed her own method. By holding up one photograph and placing it next to another, it was possible to note a star's brightness, as well as compare any changes in its brightness over time.

Some stars that Henrietta observed are called variable stars. A variable star is a star whose brightness changes from bright to dim, and back again, over time. Henrietta especially studied one type of variable star: the Cepheid variables. By careful observation of the Cepheids, she discovered a direct relationship between the time it took a star to go from bright to dim to how bright it actually was.

Henrietta's discovery helped astronomers determine greater distances of stars than they had ever been able to before. In fact, they were later able to determine the distance of some stars up to ten *million* light-years away! One astronomer used Henrietta's discoveries to measure the size of the Milky Way. Another used her work to make a better estimate of the age of the universe.

# SOME OTHER WOMEN ASTRONOMERS

Throughout history, women were not encouraged to enter the field of astronomy, and often were not respected when they did. But that didn't stop them! Henrietta Leavitt was not the only woman who achieved great things. A few others are Caroline Herschel (1750–1848), who discovered eight comets, and Annie Jump Cannon (1863–1941), who devised the basic method for classifying the stars. In modern times, E. Margaret Burbridge has made important discoveries about galaxies and quasars, Wendy Freedman has found new ways to measure the universe's rate of expansion, and Sally Ride has traveled for NASA as the first American woman in space!

# GLOSSARY

**asteroids**: Much smaller than planets (from one mile to several hundred miles in diameter), asteroids are celestial bodies that also orbit around the Sun. They are found mainly between Mars and Jupiter.

**astronomer**: A scientist who studies planets, stars, and other objects in the universe.

**Big Dipper**: A group of seven stars that form the shape of a dipper (four outline the bowl shape and three make the handle). Other names for the Big Dipper are the Plow and the Wagon.

**Copernicus**: A great Polish astronomer who lived from 1473–1543. Copernicus discovered that the Earth rotates on its axis and revolves around the Sun.

**cosmic dust**: Tiny particles of matter in interstellar space.

**eclipse**: An eclipse happens when one celestial body appears to partially or wholly cover another celestial body. On Earth, we can view either a solar (sun) or lunar (moon) eclipse.

**galaxy**: A large collection of stars, gases, and dust that forms a definite structure in space.

**Galileo**: An Italian scientist and early astronomer who lived from 1564–1642 and made many important discoveries.

**light-year**: The distance that light travels over a period of one year.

**Milky Way**: The galaxy in which our solar system is located.

**North Star**: The polar star, also known as Polaris, which is always in the north. This star has helped countless sailors and other travelers find their way.

**observatory**: A building that contains instruments and telescopes to help astronomers make observations of stars and planets.

**universe**: Everything that exists, including the Earth, the solar system, all galaxies, and all that they contain.

**variable star**: A star that periodically becomes brighter or darker because of internal or external changes in its condition.

## EXPLORE THE STARS—AND MORE!

### Astronomy, stars, space travel!
### Here are some places to land as you set out on your own space-exploring trip!

### INTERNET RESOURCES
Here are some websites where you can find information and activities:

kidsastronomy.com

astronomy.com

nasa.gov/audience/forkids/kidsclub/flash/index.html

Astronomy Picture of the Day: apod.nasa.gov/apod/

goodsitesforkids.org/Astronomy.htm

### BIBLIOGRAPHY
If you would like to read more about Henrietta Leavitt, please look at:

Johnson, George. *Miss Leavitt's Stars: The Untold Story of the Woman Who Discovered How to Measure the Universe* (New York: W. W. Norton & Company, Inc.), 2005.


More books:

Bullock, Linda. *Looking Through a Telescope (Rookie Read-About Science)* (New York: Scholastic), 2003.

Carson, Mary Kay. *Exploring the Solar System: A History with 22 Activities* (Chicago: Chicago Review Press, Inc.), 2006.

Driscoll, Michael and Meredith Hamilton. *A Child's Introduction to the Night Sky: The Story of the Stars, Planets, and Constellations—and How You Can Find Them in the Sky* (New York: Black Dog & Leventhal Publishers, Inc.), 2004.

Panchyk, Richard and Buzz Aldrin. *Galileo for Kids: His Life and Ideas, 25 Activities* (For Kids series) (Chicago: Chicago Review Press, Inc.), 2005.

Rusch, Elizabeth. Illustrated by Guy Francis. *The Planet Hunter: The Story Behind What Happened to Pluto* (Flagstaff: Rising Moon Books), 2007.

Wadsworth, Ginger. Illustrated by Craig Orback. *Benjamin Banneker: Pioneering Scientist (On My Own Biography)* (Minneapolis: Carolrhoda Books, Inc.), 2003.

An interesting monthly magazine about astronomy and the stars is *Astronomy* magazine, published in Waukesha, Wisconsin.